YOU DARLING THING

Also by Monica Ferrell

Poetry
Beasts for the Chase

Fiction
The Answer Is Always Yes

YOU DARLING THING

MONICA FERRELL

Four Way Books
Tribeca

Library of Congress Cataloging-in-Publication Data

Names: Ferrell, Monica, author.
Title: You darling thing / Monica Ferrell.
Description: New York, NY : Four Way Books, [2018]
Identifiers: LCCN 2018003717 | ISBN 9781945588228 (pbk. : alk. paper)
Subjects: LCSH: Courtship--Poetry. | Marriage--Poetry.
Classification: LCC PS3606.E7535 Y68 2018 | DDC 811/.6--dc23
LC record available at https://lccn.loc.gov/2018003717

This book is manufactured in the United States of America and printed on acid-free paper.

Four Way Books is a not-for-profit literary press. We are grateful for the assistance
we receive from individual donors, public arts agencies, and private foundations.

This publication is made possible with public funds from the New York State Council on the Arts, a
state agency.

PROUD MEMBER

[clmp]

We are a proud member of the Community of Literary Magazines and Presses.

CONTENTS

NOTES

"Oh, you sweetheart!" said Vronsky, approaching the horse and coaxing her. But the closer he came, the more excited she grew. Only when he came to her head did she suddenly quiet down, her muscles quivering under her thin, tender skin. . . . The horse's excitement had communicated itself to Vronsky; he felt the blood rushing to his heart and, like the horse, he wanted to move, to bite; it was both terrifying and joyful.

—Leo Tolstoy

Strong or weak point

You were always ready to fall to your knees!
Yes, I was always ready to fall to my knees.

—Czeslaw Milosz

THE DATE

This time we'll come gloved & blind-
folded, we'll arrive on time.

With bees in our hair,
with an escort of expiring swans.

We'll appear to out-of-date & out-of-tune
violin music, we'll lie on our side.

Wearing rotting lotus behind our ears,
musk between our thighs.

This time we'll be tied down.
We'll cry out.

We'll only smoke if surprised
by tragedy's approach, as it noses closer.

This time we'll fall in love
with the blood color

of the sunset as we're walking home
over the bridge that takes us

between *here* & *there*.
This time we'll forget

how ancient Sarmatian lions go on
bearing marble messages for no one

who can understand their sarcophagus language,
forget sloths who climb so slow

they die before mating.
We'll grow improvident & stop believing

there was ever such a thing
as *alone*, such a hard

nail in the coffin
for one.

THE WAVES

Old men on fourth-story balconies stare down at me,
Children pass by playing ball.
A mother takes in her plain tablecloth, frowning.

                                       I will die
If before nightfall no one touches me.

There is a hospital in this town called *Gli Incurabili,*
They will take me there and lay me down on the bed like an ivory blade.
I will be pure as a virgin offering empty hands to Christ
And the world will throb beneath me like sea's blue beneath its white.

IN THE FETUS MUSEUM

White, incorruptible, a slip of moon
filming the reed-bordered waters of a pond,
he sits, or rather slumps, against the glass.
He's in no hurry. The world is here,

now and then it drags up an agonized eye
to plead with him—Mahavir, tiny Nero.
Gently, almost wincing, he smiles
as though waiting for me to finish my sentence.

Unborn. A door through which possibility
never walked. Flute no one ever played.
Once his cells were assembling their lace,
his mother was blinking into the sunlight.

Perhaps his invitation was lost in the mail,
though perhaps it's just as well. After all,
he's not missing much—except everything.
The inventions of lust, the pageantry of *what*.

ANATOMY

Man shaped out of mud
And made to speak and love—
Let's stick in him a little whisperer,

A bucket with two holes.
Let's give him the Great Deceiver,
A blood-stone.

A church with a vaulted ceiling
Where the White and Blue Niles meet.
A dog who cries after dark.

Everyone has a heart,
Even the people who don't.
It floats up like a beached whale in the autopsy.

The heart has no sense of humor.
It offers itself piteously like a pair of handcuffs
And is so clumsy that we turn away.

The past
Is a quarryful of marble statues
With heads and genitals erased,

But the heart is a muscle made of sharkbone and mutters,
Resting place softened with hay
Where all the cows come, finally, home.

SAVAGE BRIDE

You need me like ice needs the mountain
On which it breeds. Like print needs the page.
You move in me like the tongue in a mouth,
Like wind in the leaves of summer trees,
Gust-fists, hollow except of movement and desire
Which is movement. You taste me the way the claws
Of a pigeon taste that window ledge on which it sits,
The way water tastes rust in the pipes it shuttles through
Beneath a city, unfolding and luminous with industry.
Before you were born, the table of elements
Was lacking, and I as a noble gas floated
Free of attachment. Before you were born,
The sun and the moon were paper-thin plates
Some machinist at his desk merely clicked into place.

PONY

After the snakebite, I tried to make noises
     With the clouds in my throat, the dissolving
Snow of my tongue: but the young ones
     Kept crying and calling and couldn't hear me.

How could I have explained anyway my surprise?
     Not the kiss of the branding iron,
Not the crop's electric shock, the bit's silver
     Felt ever as sweet to me as his firm teeth.

Decline is a river you fall into, your hind legs
     Unsteady on the slippery bank.
Your last sight a spray of delicious gillyflowers
     Bright enough to be suns.

There's so much you realize you'll never miss.
     Mornings in the sludgy mist. The saddle hours.
The way children comb and braid your mane
     Then look at you as though for repayment.

In the ring, on the bridle path, how enormous I
     Was floating above them while they rode me
As I practiced the art of surrender,
     Holding my thoughts separate as a kite—

I might as well have been on my own planet of dust,
　　Forever careering through shadow fields
Till I saw those eyes sparking green from the dark,
　　Till I let him shake my body with one touch.

OH YOU ABSOLUTE DARLING

You are sexier than anyone I've ever met.
You feel better to touch than anyone I've ever met.
You're like a Vargas girl.
You're not exactly a barrel of laughs
so much as a barrel of erections.
Dear Gypsy-themed Barbie doll:
those jeans will do you no good.

If I were a mosquito, I'd suck
all the blood out from you in five minutes.
If we were stranded together on a desert island,
I don't think you'd last long.
I'd like to come over there and squeeze the living daylights out of you.
I'd like to spin you like a top
and fuck you ten different ways.
Such tender meat—*raw*—dropping from the bone!

You're sex on a stick.
You're a sex bomb.
You're the sex symbol of our set.
And this is why you have the male friends
you think you do, why women hate you.
The last twelve years, you have *no idea*

how many millions of haploid gametes I've spilled in your honor!
How I've resented you for walking around
as though you were a normal person.

I'm sorry to break it to you.
Let me explain how this works: when X said
he threw away your press photo, what he meant was
it's tacked up in his bathroom right now, for inspiration.
I think you think my attraction to you is funny.
Believe me, scared is how you should be.

You're a basket of sexual fruits.
What kind of fruit are you?
I'd like to eat you up with my penis
but I don't know how to do that!
You smell like peach. You smell like mango.
The way you smell drives me crazy,

the divots in your back drive me wild.
I love the scoop above your ass—your slender throat—
your little pretty limbs and princess-face—
your gorgeous rippling muscles covered
all over by this smooth, this tawny upholstery—
little doll—delicate flower—the way your ribs

stick out, it's like a second rack—and this,
I love *this*: what do people call it?

You should always be naked.
You should always hold your wineglass like so.
You have what no one else has—breasts
that demand to be taken notice of
and the tiniest waist I've ever seen.
If your waist were any smaller, you wouldn't exist.

POETRY

There is nothing beautiful here
However I may want it. I can't
Spin a crystal palace of this thin air,
Weave a darkness plush as molefur with my tongue
However I want. Yet I am not alone
In these alleys of vowels, which comfort me
As the single living nun of a convent
Is comforted by the walls of that catacomb
She walks at night, lit by her own moving candle.
I am not afraid of mirrors or the future
—Or even *you*, lovers, wandering cow-fat
And rutting in the gardens of this earthly verge
Where I too trod, a sunspot, parasol-shaded,
Kin to the trees, the bees, the color green.

THE TOURIST BRIDE

At the end of the night a poisonous star
Rises above Petersburg like a cancer-spot.

Cats, fevered, untranslatable,
Go long ways for secrets and fish heads.

Amorists hide in the alcoves
Of the swollen city, guarding their possessions;

I feel the feral marble machine of my heart
Leak mercury, my veins warm

When I hear two lovers twittering
In the chalice of their arms . . . *There is something*

Deliciously final about you, she says,
I cannot say what it is.

I cannot say who you are, he says,
Remind me.

INVENTION OF THE BRIDE

At dusk words float,
Blue-fingered, without weight
In a world gone fragrant
As a gold egg cradling rose-pink yolk.

Timid at first, stilled like deer at a lake,
Now they gather to me, who pretends sleep,
Covering my face with their hands.

In the memory palace, the dead
Take short breaths.
Shamans breathe a name for who I am.
Shamans litany me into being.

I open my cold eyes, my throat.
I enter the bath, let the waters
Close over me like a gem,

Then reach for my anklet,
My red bolt of silk.
The sun rises.
From the mysterious generosity of a mother,

The sun rises.
—This time I will not be false, this time, I will be
Clear from all falsehood like a snake from its last season's skin.

GLACIER

Every sixteen-year-old girl likes
A murderer for an admirer, his eyes on her from the hotel's

Third-floor balcony as she lugs her skis from the slope.
    His gaze slits wool and cotton as she walks,

                Safety-razor-sharp along the thigh.
    His words have stubbed in her
                    Radiant suns.

Wonders what it would be like,
    Whether her parents would find her first

In morgue-light, the eyelids turned
Astonishingly exact, final,
                Attendants circulating about the table,
                    Their rubber soles squeaking.

    One gets cut in that kind of blizzard,
    Fiberglass in the lungs.

The man in question, never apprehended,
    Is sensitive, & likes her hair pulled back.

She stays away, though not too far to see
                    Blue eyes open toward her through the mercury air
Cornflower blue, blue of lasers, malevolent as the circles

            Of gas on a stove, as the blue kiss on the matchstick
                        That drags a house down.

        One time she walked into the glacier's
                    Fog-storm, Catherine wheel

Of swirling white and moan as all the while

                Crevasses yawned under her feet
        Invisibly. No one would ever find her
                    Hanging like crystals in a cave forever.

It's as though she wants to spell
                    A sentence in the book of infinity,
        To be the one child who doesn't come home
                    When her mother's setting dinner plates at dusk.

THE HOUR OF SACRIFICE

You are alone before they kill you.
Sacred before they kill you.
Barbaric and speechless as a bear,
you are a bear parting the forests

out of hunger. You have hands
for eyes, and you have a fine wire
where your mind should be—humming
with voices that shuttle their whispers

perpetually along its shining metal.
You are forsaken before they find you
as a music box lost in the rubble
of a ruined city, long after the child

who owned it has died, and when
they find you you are more forsaken still.
Because they will open and chew
something so precious they don't understand,

because they have forgotten in their histories
what it means—a magic seed.
Because they have forgotten, you cannot
be betrayed. There is no one to know

that betrayal but you, and you are busy
putting out your eyes, putting poison
below the trapdoor of your tongue,
that door which opens always to inwardness.

Child, you are alive now and your heart
beats low. The smallest drum in this place,
in this apartment empty on the far side
of the city. There is still time

to heave out of here and vanquish your enemies,
biblically, with epic bloodshed,
time to call down the curses of the world
upon their wretched heads, but you let

the moment escape from you like breath,
you let it pass like clouds over the face
of a mirror, which afterward forgets
such an event ever existed.

It's as if you are waiting. Like I said,
you are alone before they find you,
in this empty apartment on the city's far side,
listening to the smallest drum sputter and cry.

LAUDANUM

Girls will wait in meadows hoping to catch unicorns,
Conceiving a thirst that begins and ends in your body,

Drinking its pale flesh. The way they put their hands
Together, in prayer—it is like a corset: the whittled

Stone in the vial of a whale. Someone shall put an ivory
Conversion in a box. Another will whisper of lace,

Spoons. They are all listening for the small moment
When the temple's last stair falls into the sea,

Herons begin their landing. In the kingdom of a lynx-eye
The palm tree splits the rock, greedy for rain.

—For this is the room where the door comes close. For this
Is the limestone gallery, the well of dreams: their dormition.

THE SLEEPING HUSBAND

This massive apartment: a whole room left
Empty to air, where we used to sleep.
So many steps on the waxed wood, like off turns
On the dial of a lock whose combination one's lost—
All decaying about me like empire,
The moldings moldering while I sit frozen
As a swan on the surface of a lake changing to ice.
Fruitflies and mosquitoes, a water bug,
Carpet beetles, the mouse found behind the couch
Months after it'd shrunk to a puff of fur:
Nothing to eat here but beer and more dark.
The shower where someone's young wife died
In an explosion of epilepsy while he slept.
One wonders what he was dreaming then.
The same dreams we once made here, maybe.

BRIDE DRESSED IN FUR AND STEAM

A dream of zebras breaks up
     In the eye of morning the way the image
On a well scatters with one thrown coin.
     I've said before, I don't mind living alone.

All night, rope-bridges, tablas, hard
     Wicker settees, a man with a gun
But I got rid of his body neatly
     And no one knew, a locomotive

Steam and old-fashioned as *Anna Karenina,*
     A platform, destinations on the placard
And no one knew. The man's eyes turn
     Up in the head of a hound, black pools

Infinite as the rings of Saturn. See,
     Even in dreams I get the job done:
I didn't skip a beat, walking serenely
     To the train—I might have been in furs,

A stole, white, very clean—since I knew
     Everything here was accomplished in justice
For what had been done to me,
     No one anymore could touch me.

IN THE FETUS MUSEUM

You tiny Nero among peacock silks: you mother-
of-pearl-handled pistol, you mill of stillness
swaddled by dazzling chemistry petals,
shut up in a Mason jar—what are you
listening to, Brown-eye? Is that a smile?
Maybe right now you're dreaming of some distance,
heavens shaped from white, marmoreal fields
where your dead mother's frozen, witch-finger touch
finds your body, finally. It's not too different
outside: here, love is a currency everyone wants.
Where I am, you can't get enough of touch
and the sun is a bloom who drowns each night,
air is like that wine you sleep in. We walk around
on two legs, going places. I have a kite
in my chest I take out at times to fly.

EMMA BOVARY

I would have liked then for someone to touch me
So I could know the purpose of this hardship.
Black-eyed and impassive as a canyon,
From the hive of my mind, I looked at their faces
As I moved between rows of espaliered pears.
I only intended for someone to show
Me, once, an affection like the sun
Shows even the simplest bulb, entering what's hidden.
Let me show them instead the picture
In a knife's reflection, take down my hair
Where the gravedigger kneels among new potatoes.
Behind my teeth are headstones, and behind those
Skeletons of cavemen, of dinosaurs,
And under my skin: alphabets, alphabets
In black ink, a legacy of histories tiny and alive
As an ant army marching toward forever.
Understand, please—I, too, have a splendid use,
This world could not get rid of me if it wanted to.

PLANET

You're alive. You stumble from the spaceship's hull
Testing your radio . . . it gives a promising fuzz,
But the mother-craft does not return your call.
So you're forced to find food and water,

Though the food here is green, the water purple.
Furtively you try them, one night, cursing,
Ravenous, on a hillock, under pale, circling moons—
Sweetness of daffodils, water crisp as dimes.

Still you're searching for some key thing:
Minerals? Fuel? At the time you like to call midnight,
Long spokes of smoke rise from mountain pools
And when the violet sun gashes you awake

You see how everyone on earth is retreating from you
The way starfish slide beneath soft, repeated waves.
What a distant country is human touch; and good riddance.
Scrambling over the cliffs of your new planet,

Strange but not unpleasant, with angular black rocks,
Periodically you may gasp, checking over a shoulder
But then you'll recall *there is no one else here,*
No one else in this world, and carry on with your roving.

L'HEURE VERTE

Mornings you are the ruins of yourself,
Green calcite. Where the eyes dried,
Two black rooks lie nesting in the grooves
Worn smooth by thousands of hands
Groping toward the brilliant ocean.
Near the bottom of your hollow mouth,
Your cut tongue gathers lizard scales
Like a sunken bucket in an algal well.
Well, well. You've learned your lesson
This time, haven't you? All the monks
Have died, in their single-cell caves
On the mountainside, their rice-bowls
Overturned. What you so often think
Belongs to you does not belong to you at all.

AQUARIUM

As so many ears opening, then squeezing shut
    greedily upon news of something long expected
that, having come, turns out not important,
    meek companies of effulgent jellyfish
soar through floodlit rays of brilliant cobalt.
    Fists of inwardness who unclench to grasp
at the glassed-in blue that sieves through, they hiccup,
    bloom. Umbrellas buoyed by an updraft,
bridal veils dangling lace strings of bubbles, they rise,
    then sink softly: a numinous snowfall, the ghosts
of underwear that fell to floors centuries before,
    trailing filaments of ribbons in their wake.
They'll never see the sun or speak a word.
    Desire keeps rippling their transparent skin.

INVENTION OF THE BRIDEGROOM

Wait by the rocks and take up your knitting.
Let your smell waft out of that briny tang—
just give it time, little siren, patience.
Wait by the rocks long enough, and he will show.
First he'll blindfold you; then he'll slip the gag
into your mouth: all there's left to do is lie
down on your side till he gets the binds tight.
After all, his hands know what they need,
they can find it even in the far darkness where you are.
What a childhood of wasps taught him this . . .
For a moment, he almost looks happy.
But already, like a moon slipping over
the horizon, the end arrives. Then his cry:
bleak and lonely, a lost boat's foghorn bleating.

HAREM SONG

Blue crocuses cincture the snake's hole.
                Monkeys in the palms gibber, wild.

By midnight we'll be drunk or high
                When he arrives with the smile

Of a man who's just gotten away with murder.
                White peacocks shake their tails and strut.

Say *Effendi*, say *Pearl-of-the-Pure-of-Heart* if he chooses you
                Or just open your mouth, as though in surprise.

White peacocks panic in the tall ferns, the reeds.
                If he can't get it up, he'll fall

Asleep in your lap as though it were history.
                Listen: that's the oud player tuning up.

I don't want to tell you how to do this,
                But you might think about a little kohl,

A few jewels. You might take a look
                At whatever's happening with your bust.

The oud player coughs when our lord can't get it up,
        Ivy in the pool comes apart.

Somewhere a mutiny is tearing loose from
        Its tree like ripe fruit;

But as for now, little boarder, orphan, we're here in this pavilion
        Briefly, this galley-deep and portholed

Place called Earth and you must row your bit,
        Sister: see how lovely you are in the mirror.

You must consider: it was the Will. Your beauty. It was the shiny
        Machine

Made a garden of Eden in your veins, and paradise
        Of your soft sigh.

THE KING WITH HIS QUEEN

My victory, my triumph, my memory, my fabulous
Speed, my kingdom, my forest fire, my pure
Flash flood in a thimble. My morning orison,
My dovecote, my insurrection, my soaked
Bales of hay, my great bane. Throbbing, ruinous thing,
You scent of autumn and its dark bowl, whose waters

Brim over everything and change it all to bone. My
Excellent marksman, my kennels' guard who feeds the starving
Scores and plucks out their motes—
They blink and, overcome by gratefulness,
Say nothing, just like your hands, my sister
In hospice, at midnight with black dress trailing.

Let me tell you your funeral in the pewter rain
Was like holding my breath and with quiet tread
Following into the room where you were
Dressing, vapor in the old blind mirror. Love,
All the messages brought down by your gold-
Throated angels have come out garbled and rot,

Tell me one five-letter word how I may survive
This era of red leaves, the poaching season
Without my Chief of the Hunt. Without my legion,

My bowl of ocean, my delicious crystal
Chess piece who always captured her beleaguered king.
You were my lake's smile as it rises out of darkness

Under the burgeoning stars—and still, my candelabra's
One stubborn wick: when all the porters are down the hall dozing
And the castle hardens into a hard knot of blood
Aching to pass through the contracted valve—you are
The dance of shadows in the drunken room
And its invitation with outstretched fingers.

BEATRICE D'ESTE

When you consider all I have left behind,
The ermine muffs, glasses that sang out like sirens
At a finger's tap, argent fish traveling
Upon gilt plates like ruptured silk or mercury,
When you recall my long afternoons, sunlight
Trailing along the floor like heavy velvet,
My pearl-crusted carriage, jester, my guitar,

What should I miss? Remember, I was also a mother,
Two seahorses once swam out from my ocean.
I was even devoted. I hovered like a cloud
At the cribs' edge, watching their limbs grow tight.
Day after day, my white face played parasol
Sheltering those saplings and the fantastic dreams
Assembling on their bodies' trunks like greenery.

And yet only dregs of that elixir stain my glass,
All that has faded, gone from me in heat;
Now I wonder: what were they truly, so young
They could not return the river of my love
But a couple of trembling puppies, blindly licking?
I have washed my hands of such salt. The thing
I miss came earlier. It's simple, really:

The first night my lord laid me down in our bed
He slit me wide as a flower's green calyx.
Then, bending back my branches for grafting,
Skillfully he pinned me. Later he blessed my hands
And kissed my lips like departing snowflakes
Before falling back on his pillow, a monument
Of impassive sandstone I knew to leave alone.

Watching him snore, at first I felt hurt
But then a girlish filament of fire
Made my whole body flame. Do you see?
Lying there in the sheets, my body beaten
Thinner than gold leaf, I had become bodiless
Vapor, a musical note, a vanishing point or door:
He had used me so completely I was seen through.

BEAUTIFUL FUNERAL

Tonight, you are thinking of heroin,
Of the boy who pulled you to his lips
In a blue room and whispered *heroin*
So close you could feel it on your face like a cloudburst.

He makes you think of furs and Russia,
Midnight sun and Petersburg canals, a sullen gun
Where one bullet's lodged like something in the craw
Of a drowned boy fished from beneath docks.

His limbs were white with blue veins
Spidered beneath the light shell of his skin
Open to the littlest bark, the tiniest trireme,
His veins were vulnerable as a bruise-black mare

Just as the barn begins to spark. And once
In the night that held its candle closer to see
His needled flesh heaved beneath the sink
Of a city bathroom, aching to vomit up its ore . . .

You would have dusted off those peacock rings
Below his eyes with your sandpaper tongue,
Lapped his form in camphor-drenched gauze
Then washed him in waves of organ music.

You would have pressed down that black key
By his spine's base to hear the deepest of tones
A body can moan. Ah, invalid.
We would have made a beautiful funeral.

PHYSICAL

I am older now and my eyesight is getting better,
but I confess my lungs and heart are shot.
Someone could drive me in a pickup out to the lake
and push me in, I wouldn't even complain
as I floated out, arms extended, tangling in milfoil
and puzzlegrass and the rusted-out remains
of vehicles that passed into sleep years ago.
The body is a temple and in this body

I have sown a lot of dark. I have sown seeds of want,
they looked like dried sand dollars but were soft
and opened up afterwards inside.
My body was a factory for crystal ichors
that came out through my eyes and were caught
by the thirsty hands of air. My tongue was a rowboat,
it rowed me across silences,
then sat empty and useless, wooden in a corner.

I breathed dust, dust till my people
could make bricks from its inexhaustible supply.
And what was the point of all that industry, Doctor?
What once was valuable went wrecked with use
and nobody got any richer. The world's wealth
is finite as oil, and every body finally

gives way to nightmares that scatter fast as clouds.
Yet every day I'm at it, hammer and tongs,

working the mind's loom and the bellows of the lungs,
feeding all the dogs in the kennel of my heart,
oh down to the newest and littlest one.
And here you sit with your stethoscope and that
blip-blip meant to measure my electricity,
how it mounts and wanes irregular as waves
crossing a fathomless ocean for no reason
other than that's where they will go.

Surely there must be times you doubt your oath.
What is physical is what is natural, which is to say,
in either case: it wants to give birth to more,
more, spewing out shrimps and runts of the litter
and lacelike microbes in an endless parade
which no one is watching, I suppose, save God.
There is the *here*, and there is the *now*, and
at the place they intersect in an x-marks-the-spot

there is sometimes also a little bubble called *breath*,
and when the bubble is present we call this *life*,
if it bursts we call this that other, the dark country.

Surely there must've been times when you touched
the fragrant, frangible edge of that bubble
and wanted nothing more than to puncture it?
When the metal of your instruments sang in your ears
like the serpents who licked Hippocrates' clear

till all you could hear was the language of the deathless
and, beneath that, their approach.

THE LAST WOLF IN ST. PETERSBURG

Imagine the violet eyes alight in its wild face:
Waterways silvered over with fading midnight sun.

Once all that was was wolves'. And then with shotguns
Nobles cleared the place, the furred gray

Falling to the dirt in bloodied bits—
The swamps drained, the woods

Cut and their sap-dried amber tacked on to palace
Walls as papering.
                    In the exquisite

Picture-book I have of the sport, maps are drawn,
Diagrams for how to peel back the skin,

And nail it down to dry in neat sections
Marked with the names of pelt territories

Like an atlas of the new found world. Heaven
Is like that, they say, hierarchical, ordained.

IN THE FETUS MUSEUM

With just the indentation of a line
Where an eye should have come to the fore
And an impress, an inch-length wrinkle
For his unopening mouth, near pinpricks
Which dictate in faint constellations whiskers
That never formed—seed-points, God's dots
Left unconnected on such paper—the world's
Smallest white dog sits gamely in his glass cage,
Closed off by its dark fluid from all change
Like Laika left trailing in space, that moon room
Where everything is backward, broken, erased
As bridges lifted on the Neva, your diffident
Silence to my last letter, or that breath which stops
My saying what swims me too, unhurt and whole.

BETROTHAL

Small jolts animate the corpse of my body:
I discover my gut, my thigh, light in my throat.
Now I am immortal and made of wrung silk,
moving effortlessly as the haunches of horses.

Here, in bar-glow, you're like a ripple of ink
that turns the night darker where you are,
slicker. I could fit my tongue into your gaze
and drink. I could put my finger in your mouth.

We circle each other the way flecks of dirt
together revolve toward a sink's metal hole.
Your apartment's round the corner, I know.
We only have the rest of our lives.

EPITHALAMIUM

Night creaked about them like a game of chairs;
They looked for safety and again and again
Clung to the eroding island of each other.

Pale blue, their shipwreck eyes beseeched us
Like eyes of Christian martyrs at the circus—
Still, no one wanted to talk to the newlyweds.

WAKING

Gradually, they become aware of their bodies.
But they cannot move them, they are underwater
like lilies whose tendrils have got snared
on something sunken, the rusted blade of a plow.
In the girl's mind, thought is falling like sand
through the clear waist of an hourglass;
above the boy's head, in the hinged clock,
a dozen toothed gears go on whirring—
while outside, the white light gathers, growing huge
as an ocean whose rising tide
dissolves the letter dropped in a high basin . . .
till they can't even remember their names
anymore, they can't believe they used to touch
each other in sleep or cry out with what felt like love.

BRIDE OF THE FALSE COIN

When I take my scissors to your shirts,
I am frightened: not that they will whimper
But that they won't understand the violence I mean.
That kind of violence is the other side of love,

Bright as a lightsaber and permanent
As the angels' swords above Eden
Barring that couple with a final X,
That violence means a love strong as death.

Once *Sie ist mein Leben*, you said, meaning me
And I took those words personally
And knocked upon the door of my heart
Until all its birds flooded to you, in a rush—

Like a sachem, I tugged on our calumet,
I wrote your name in smoke. Then went home
With my pockets rolling in shining glass beads,
My pockets so rich with the coin of your country.

HELIOPAUSE

After a vase breaks, after
the shatter, how silence holds its ear
to the floor, waiting for one of us to speak.
After the door slams, or a car drives off.
There's only interstellar void beyond,

as it was before we met.
So, slowly we'll return to what we were
as though the other had never been born,
our bodies never touched.
There is a rim, an end to everything.

In particular, fields, magnetic fields
and floating atoms, and storms,
storms that produce spirals
rose in color, folded
like a "ballerina's skirt"

and local galactic charge, and time,
no, not time, but winds
blown out so far by the sun
as though our sun were blowing
a bubble, chewing gum

while always its influence diminishes
against the winds of other stars
till at last, as when two hands part,
when the ghost of the other can no longer be felt
and love is an object only for memory,

"termination shock," waves of it,
still everything halts at an edge—
that place where the sun won't reach.
Believe me, even if it takes thousands of years
I will forget your face

THE LACE WORLD

How eerie it all is, as if linked by synapses;
a face stutters out of the cloud of lace,
a tiny decorative lion dances in a frieze,
a woman, needy arms outstretched, holds on

to thread bulwarks against some unseen flood
while her body dissolves into netting, the knots
widen and widen until the limn of her
is finished, she melted to loops of distance . . . and isn't

that how *you've* transformed, once-love, while
this strait sleeping car, this *time*
spirits me away from you and that night we lay
two palms folded to each other in prayer:

how the cat yowled to be let in! and the moths,
darting abortively forward, all ended up
by clinging to the screen in the sleep-sacs
of their wings, while I rolled to the top of my tongue

that word which would end everything and
like Sisyphus, let it fall.
                              Nothing
brings that second back, yet nothing gets lost;

hours that separate me from you only
tighten the memory-chain, where my thoughts
like these light acrobats trapeze:
in the white spiderwebbing, in the network

here's a sea serpent, a helmeted soldier,
a boy pausing to sing, two dogs leaving a fountain,
someone pushing aside a harp.
The tiny *o* of her mouth. Those gouged-out holes, her eyes.

ARACHNE

"A god can do it"—yes. But a girl?
The Greeks named it *hubris*,
As if she had a choice: this is all
She knows how to be. Someone gave this *weaving*
Into her keeping, she must let it play out.

There she is, the contest is over, there she is
Turning away from the frame: as if
Expecting applause, searching out
Her mother in the audience. But already
She feels it overtaking her. She understands.

How softly her head drops to one shoulder,
As if listening, or asking herself,
How long has it been since I was happy?
Mostly she is tired now, she has not
Slept for days. She used to sleep so well.

Watch her fingers, still touching what has been
Woven, as if feeling for an opening—
Slowly all the beauty in them is frozen.
Nothing will loosen them again. Yet how
Abstracted she is, only absent-mindedly herself,

She has *finished* with it. We can go inside.
Where is the famous justice of jealous Athena,
Her merciful thirteenth vote? In the end
The gods are all paper and bronze, heartless.
They have not yet been told about love.

THE TIGER ABANDONED AT THE HUNT'S END

1.

Blind and tiny, I awoke
In this world in the dark,
My mother's lullabies were the muttering of reeds.

Shrouded in palm fronds,
Helpless breather in a nest of fur
I nursed.

The children of men dream of me.

I grew, titanic
Building of meat.

My first word was *darkness*
My second
Teeth.

2.

What is it simmers through jungle breeze
What cries red through vestibules of cells
But inveterate hunger
One moment it's for death,
The next love
So these two confuse . . .

There was a home for me once, beyond
Gullies of water I hardly recall now
That I stalk the orchards of farness,
Invulnerable and orphaned as the night.

3.

Precious precious precious
What can be taken in the mouth.
Delicious the mouth
Delicious the paws, oh God, throbbing—

Slender death, you make your way for me,
Sleek and sinuously bending,
Breakless curves
I hear over my shoulders
As I separate the body from the body
When I sit to the miracle of kill,
Going deeper into the wound.

4.

Often we'll hear them, men.
See their flames' spluttering on hills.
It isn't hard to avoid their clumsy craven traps,
Bird-lime—and what they do to bridges,
Widening those slats and placing stakes
On which they hope we'll impale ourselves
By the force of our own fantastic weight.

No, it isn't hard at all. But sometimes, nonetheless, the call of
Loneliness rang out the sweetest-sounding
Bird in my forest

5.

So it came for me with a rain of sulfur and sparks—
Fireworks scattering daylight, floods of
Sunspots of blood drowning
All the friends, my younger selves—
Down on one leg.
Down on my side.
Hammered down.
Iron. Then,
The woman stiffly lifted from her horse,
The man planting his rifle in the ground . . .
Proud, the coward!

Lying on my back, I widened my eyes
Till they were as wide as the sky
And in that sky there was whiteness
Like the whiteness at the end of the mind

I felt my body wilt like snow
I felt it blow away like clouds
I was all heart and eyes
I couldn't even use my mouth
The ground was swimming in me

Breeze was swimming in me
Memories lifted from my body like flies

I thought, *Thank God,*
It is as serious as I always knew it should be.
I thought, *Black door.*
We all understood what was on the other side.

From a distance, the woman watched
Her man approach me,
Bend his gaze over me,
Blue with reverence and affection,
Blue a listening ear blue a set of arms
Fixed and stern enough to hold me,
Blue that knows what it is for me to give
My whole self up in surrender
And I fell in love, ah
My bridegroom
Irretrievably and always, till long
After I heard your boots' steps fade away from this place.

BRIDE OF RUIN

You've always had a thing for cities like this,
For their deserted wells, the grass-padded flagstones
Going nowhere, and all these splayed mosaics
Where thin-limbed bathers once frolicked and fucked
Spattered by birdshit beneath florid trees.
You're a ruined town too, or nearly,
Hair dissolving to gray, still every month your womb
Spits out another *no*, coughs up its mouthful of blood.
Did you love men so much you couldn't choose
Or love them so little you didn't care?
No one remembers and it hardly matters now
Whether it took war or blight or plague, God
Or betrayal to bring the stupid people
Of Aphrodisias down in their catastrophe.

A FUNFAIR IN HELL

While the proprietor looms at the center of the bar
in white linen suit, as though on safari,
I trace the grooves worn in this old wood,
I taste my beer and it is cold as some god.

The lights in hell must be something like these,
immortal as remorse, as words once they are spoken,
and the people in hell must be like these men
holding engines of heads spinning emptily in their hands.

The proprietor wears a flickering smile
pretty as the word *syphilis*.
He shines one beer tap, then another.
The silence in my mouth is a piece of felt.

I am ready for my annunciation, Angels.
I am ready for the enormity.
Bring out the unguents, the strigil and gauze.
Weigh my heart against a feather.

THE BRIDE IN WINTER

Snowflakes falling on the beaten copper of nightwater,
Filling up the mouths of drowned soldiers,
Snowflakes filling the sidewalk cracks,
Edging the trees with a blue light.

Snowflakes are indifferent as balloons,
Bridges that cross in space but go nowhere.
Like the legs of insects, they are finned with complicated shapes
Falling through a black that is atmosphere

In lines eternal as Genghis Khan's caravan across Asia,
As Napoleon forever gathering his troops in a hollow of bone:
For a long time the soldiers waited, guns in their hands,
But that white did not relinquish the sky.

Yes, the newspapers are right:
Snow is general over this part of the world,
It is falling softly on the paving slates and the well-wrought sea,
Softly falling on everything past, happening, and to come.

Once I welcomed you into my house.
Your hands were lit coals
Fixed on my back;
Goodbye to all that.

Oh silver flashes of mercury, of manna,
Falling on the house of the girl who waits by the window,
Falling on the branches that will snap,
Dazzling hypnotism—seraglio of deficient stars!

THE BRIDE STRIPPED BARE BY HER BACHELORS, EVEN

1.

All night I lay in the strange bed.

2.

You fell asleep in the temple as a boy
Woke up with a heart of stone.

3.

Does the budding break the branch and does this
Hurt?

4.

What's conceivable and what's happened lie side by side:
A corpse and a badly-sized coffin.

5.

We stayed here on the sidewalk, waiting
For the man with rabbits to come by.

6.

I do not hope to meet his face anymore.
I have turned his body into a cold and rigid door.

7.

We stayed late and took down our hair
Endlessly.

8.

hunting horns, dog collars,
hound tethers, gamenooses

9.

Endlessly

OF THE IRRESOLUBLENESS OF DIAMONDS

If my love for you were a teacup,
I would praise it for its blue. I'd consider
Its delicate handle, the pictures painted there
Of ladies, of their parasols.
But my love is not a teacup,

It is not even the tar pit from which we draw
Fodder for the desolate streets, oh lightless at night,
Oh pathways asking for feet and their memory,
It is not even a tugboat going
Bravely into morning, carrying cordage and salt,

Nor that saddest, sickest animal
In the zoo, carious, mangy, whose hair molts,
Who with its wounds sits in the bare
Hay-padded corner of a cell and licks
At the question of what it means to be here.

Yet in winter my love is covered with the brightness
Of snow, in winter my love is filled with eyes.
It waits for me at the block's edge,
Habitual dog, who walks me back into that gaseous
Entity we call *life*. Others' loves may wink and smile

Like the moon through a resurrection of vapors,
Like the coy and barbarous moon, who knows no allegiance.
But my love is more like an ice-sculpture
In a country of perpetual coldness, which the heat
Of your anger cannot damage, nor the pick

Of your words impugn. Now
Lay your worry aside from you, stranger,
Put your hands near these curves: do you feel
That hallowed temperature? Among my people
We call this *absolute love.*

DAYS OF OAKLAND

Now and then, you heard the copters
Flying in search of inmates who'd escaped.
Mostly, though, it was quiet. At night, outside,
The cats would fight and fuck and knock shit down,

The couple next door would simmer in heat
Or bitterness. Sometimes you saw them,
In the window-glass, appearing
Like quarter-moons through mist.

There was a drip, of course. *Drip drip drip*
Endless in the bathtub's white expanse as Napoleon's
Soldiers entering Russia . . .
A whiteness like that is staggering!

A woman alone is a cave of violets,
A man alone a squirming rat, who squeaks. At night,
The cats would fight and fuck, at night
Inmates ran into fields of liberty and so were saved

While, obsessively, out of destitute hope,
Copters' dilated eyes went on roving . . .
It was like trying to push a mountain up a river
Or drag a body behind you with one hand.

A woman alone is fire on a mountain,
Light in darkness, nightflowers opening
Unobserved,
Releasing their scent into everywhere.

A woman alone is a shuttered garden
Heaped on the edge of a cliff.
The identity of the bridegroom is slowly revealed.
There is no turning back from that face.

NOTES

IN THE FETUS MUSEUM—these poems are after Peter the Great's collection of fetal oddities held in his Kunstkamera in St. Petersburg, the first museum in Russia.

PONY—after a poem by Alexander the Wild, a 13th-century German minnesinger. The relevant lines read: *One child walked in the tall grass, / started, and cried aloud: / "Children, right here there was a snake! / He has bitten our pony— / It will never heal, / It must always / Remain poisoned and unwell."*

OH YOU ABSOLUTE DARLING—the title is after a scene in *Anna Karenina*, where Count Vronsky directs several such endearments toward his horse as he spurs her on during a race. (At a critical jump Vronsky shifts his weight ineptly, breaking her back. The horse is shot.) The entirety of the poem's text is comprised of verbatim statements made to the author over a period of time by an erstwhile companion.

L'HEURE VERTE—"The Green Hour," a phrase used in 19th-century France to refer to the cocktail hour for absinthe-drinkers. After a sculpture by Bedřich Stefan, "Girl With Absinthe."

BEATRICE D'ESTE—one of the best-known princesses of the Italian Renaissance, Beatrice D'Este bore her husband Ludovico Sforza two sons and died, at twenty-one, giving birth to a third.

THE LAST WOLF IN ST. PETERSBURG—the wolves native to the area around St. Petersburg were efficiently and rapidly rendered all but extinct soon after the city was founded. On this subject, Eduard Jerrmann in 1852, writes, "[N]ay, so great is the scarcity of wolves at St. Petersburg, that when the court on one occasion, to pleasure a foreign prince, got up a wolf-hunt, the witty prince, when the chase was ended, expressed great surprise at the singular breed of the slain savage, round whose neck the hair was rubbed off, *exactly as if he had worn a collar*." (*St. Petersburg: Its People; Their Character and Institutions*) Even the account of Edward Morton in 1830 reveals his great disappointment on meeting with no wolves during the course of an elaborate wolf-hunt.

HELIOPAUSE—the *heliopause* is the boundary where the sun's wind is no longer powerful enough to push back the stellar winds of surrounding stars. Voyager I and II were both launched in 1977 with the mission of discovering the heliopause. In the last ten years the twin spacecraft both crossed Termination Shock, and Voyager I officially entered interstellar space in 2012.

THE LACE WORLD—after a piece of 16th-century Breton lace, artist unknown, on view in the Hermitage Museum, St. Petersburg.

BRIDE OF RUIN—located near the modern village of Geyre, about 140 miles from İzmir, the ancient city known as Aphrodisias from the 3rd-century BCE (after having been known as *Megale Polis* [Great City]) is in ruins. Archaeologists have generated numerous possible reasons for its demise, including a 7th-century CE earthquake.

A FUNFAIR IN HELL—Dutch idiom denoting a sunshower. After Vincent van Gogh's "Le Café de nuit."

THE BRIDE IN WINTER—owes phrases to the final paragraph of James Joyce's "The Dead" and the last line of W. B. Yeats's "Sailing to Byzantium."

THE BRIDE STRIPPED BARE BY HER BACHELORS, EVEN—title from Duchamp's work in the Philadelphia Museum of Art.

ACKNOWLEDGMENTS

Grateful acknowledgment is made to the editors of the following
magazines and journals, where many of these poems first appeared,
sometimes under a different title:

Academy of American Poets' Poem-a-Day Project,
American Letters & Commentary, *The Awl*, *The Baffler*,
Chronicle of Higher Education, *Failbetter*, *Guernica*,
Indiana Review, *The Indian Quarterly*, *The Literary Review*,
The Los Angeles Review of Books, *Memorious*, *Missouri Review*,
The New Republic, *The Offing*, *The Paris Review*, *Ploughshares*,
A Public Space, *The Rumpus*, *Slate*, and *Tin House*.

Some of these poems also appeared in the following anthologies:

The Bloodaxe Book of Contemporary Indian Poets;
The HarperCollins Book of Modern English Poetry by Indians;
The Hide-and-Seek Muse: Annotations of Contemporary Poetry;
*Indivisible: An Anthology of Contemporary South Asian American
Poetry*; *Isn't It Romantic: 100 Love Poems by Younger American
Poets*; *Literature: A World of Writing*; *Poem-A-Day: 365 Poems for
Every Occasion*; and *The Rumpus Original Poetry Anthology*.

I am thankful to the Civitella Ranieri Foundation for its gift of the time and space in which some of these poems were written. And to Rick Barot, Jericho Brown, Gabriel Fried, and the five Pettes, for their comradeship and the generosity of their insights.

Thank you to Four Way Books, and especially to Martha Rhodes and Ryan Murphy.

And thanks to Michael Dumanis, without whom there wouldn't be a book, and to Julian Dumanis, whose trains are on my desk as I type these words.

Born in New Delhi, India, Monica Ferrell is also the author of *Beasts for the Chase* (Sarabande, 2008), which won the Kathryn A. Morton Prize and was a finalist for the Asian American Writers' Workshop Prize in Poetry, as well as the novel *The Answer Is Always Yes* (The Dial Press/Random House, 2008), one of Booklist's Ten Best Debut Novel selections of that year. A former Wallace Stegner Fellow at Stanford University and a "Discovery"/*The Nation* prizewinner, she directs the creative writing program at Purchase College (SUNY) and lives in Brooklyn with her husband and two children.

Publication of this book was made possible by grants and donations. We are also grateful to those individuals who participated in our 2017 Build a Book Program. They are:

Anonymous (6), Evan Archer, Sally Ball, Vincent Bell,
Jan Bender-Zanoni, Zeke Berman, Kristina Bicher, Laurel Blossom,
Carol Blum, Betsy Bonner, Mary Brancaccio, Lee Briccetti,
Deirdre Brill, Anthony Cappo, Carla & Steven Carlson,
Caroline Carlson, Stephanie Chang, Tina Chang, Liza Charlesworth,
Paula Colangelo, Maxwell Dana, Machi Davis, Marjorie Deninger,
Emily Flitter, Lukas Fauset, Monica Ferrell, Jennifer Franklin,
Helen Fremont Donna Thagard, Robert Fuentes & Martha Webster,
Chuck Gillett, Dorothy Goldman, Dr. Lauri Grossman,
Naomi Guttman & Jonathan Mead, Steven Haas, Mary &
John Heilner, Hermann Hesse, Deming Holleran, Nathaniel Hutner,
Janet Jackson, Christopher Kempf, David Lee, Jen Levitt,
Howard Levy, Owen Lewis, Paul Lisicky, Sara London &
Dean Albarelli, David Long, Katie Longofono, Cynthia Lowen,
Ralph & Mary Ann Lowen, Donna Masini, Louise Mathias,
Catherine McArthur, Nathan McClain, Victoria McCoy,
Gregory McDonald, Britt Melewski, Kamilah Moon,
Carolyn Murdoch, Rebecca & Daniel Okrent, Tracey Orick,
Zachary Pace, Gregory Pardlo, Allyson Paty, Veronica Patterson,
Marcia & Chris Pelletiere, Maya Pindyck, Taylor Pitts,
Eileen Pollack, Barbara Preminger, Kevin Prufer, Vinode Ramgopal,
Martha Rhodes, Peter & Jill Schireson, Roni & Richard Schotter,
Andrew Seligsohn, Soraya Shalforoosh, Peggy Shinner, James Snyder
& Krista Fragos, Alice St. Claire-Long, Megan Staffel, Robin Taylor,
Marjorie & Lew Tesser, Boris Thomas, Judith Thurman,
Susan Walton, Calvin Wei, Abby Wender, Bill Wenthe,
Allison Benis White, Elizabeth Whittlesey, Hao Wu, Monica Youn,
and Leah Zander.